Christ The Great Physician

by Gordon and Freda Lindsay

Published by
CHRIST FOR THE NATIONS INC.
Dallas, TX
Reprint 1997

Table of Contents

How We Overcame Sickness in Our Home

The problem of sickness is one of the most serious matters a family must face. Some families are fortunate, and do not have to spend much; others have medical and hospital bills that amount to thousands of dollars. Some people, as a result of prolonged sickness in the family, have been forced to mortgage their homes to defray the cost of expensive treatments.

And the expense of being sick is only one side of the picture. There is also the fact that some people suffer years of excruciating pain, not to speak of being unable to live a normal life. Or worse, some are suddenly cut off, leaving behind grief-stricken loved ones. Physicians are often able to alleviate pain, and in some cases effect remarkable cures. Nevertheless, they themselves recognize their limitations. They can make no guarantees that their patients will recover.

Sickness often attacks without warning. Cancer may suddenly strike an otherwise healthy person. If the disease is in an early stage, surgery or treatment may stop its progress. The disease may take a person's life in a short time, though thousands of dollars are spent to secure the best help medical science has to offer. If a person is fortunate, he may recover completely. The less fortunate recover sufficiently to get around, but are unable to resume their former work or fulfill the normal responsibilities of life.

Sickness and disease are enemies of the human race. Perhaps one of the strangest delusions entertained in the name of religion is that which regards sickness as the will of God, a blessing sent in disguise. Those who teach this, however, show by their actions that they do not really believe it. For when they become ill, they invariably send for the doctor in the hope of being cured. If they practiced what they supposedly believe, would they not thank God for their sickness rather than try to evade the will of God by getting well?

The fact is, sickness is of the devil, as the Bible plainly teaches (Job. 2:7, Acts 10:38). In the following pages, we tell how God helped our family defeat sickness in our home. We believe that it will help you do the same.

We do not want to give the impression that one secures the blessings of divine healing and health without a struggle. We have been tested time and again, and on occasion have faced a desperate onslaught from the enemy. At such times, it was not the matter of some minor ailment such as a cold or a case of the flu. We have had the devil strike with the sting of death, and only by means of a miracle of God did we survive. In each case, God wrought a miracle. We have had to face such diseases as cancer. Once my aged mother suffered a stroke which affected her mind. We had a son born with crossed eyes, one eye turned inward so much that it was partially concealed by the bridge of his nose. Another child went blind in one eye. More than once death itself seemed to come into our home. Nevertheless, we are able to testify that God has never failed us. He gave us grace to bear up under each blow. He answered our prayers and brought deliverance in every case.

On the following pages, we tell the story of how God met our family in dealing with the sickness and, how He has enabled us to enjoy the blessings and benefits of healing and health. We trust that this true story will give encouragement and blessing to others. What God has done for us, He will do for you.

Ptomaine Poisoning

During my first revival campaign, which was conducted in a tent in a small city in Southern California, I was stricken with what turned out to be an almost fatal case of ptomaine poisoning. We were never quite certain what brought about the attack, but it undoubtedly resulted from something that I had eaten. My friends had gone somewhere for the day. It was about noon when severe pains began to seize me, and I lay down thinking that presently I would be better.

I shouldn't have done that, for had I taken dominion over the thing at once in the Name of the Lord, no doubt I would have secured relief. Instead, in a very short time, agonizing cramps began to strike me at brief intervals, leaving me without enough breath or strength to pray. I believe right there I made a mistake that many Christians make. Instead of rebuking the enemy when he appeared with the first symptom, I yielded to the thing; and before I realized it, Satan had secured a foothold.

When my friends returned, they saw that I was extremely ill. They and others prayed for me, but I received no visible deliverance. Rather, the cramps seemed to increase. I have no desire to exaggerate, but the suffering seemed as intense as it is possible for a human being to experience. Everyone knows how painful a brief cramp can be; but these attacks continued at intervals of a few moments over a period of two weeks!

Naturally my friends became somewhat disturbed over the fact that my condition did not improve. Some kind neighbors who attended our meetings volunteered to take me into their home. But in spite of the best possible care, I showed no improvement and steadily grew worse. I could eat nothing; the very thought of food increased my nausea.

After a few days, when they saw no sign of improvement, these good people became alarmed and insisted that a physician be called. I thank the Lord for physicians, but I must testify that as God has revealed Himself as my Great Physician, I have always felt that I must lean upon Him alone. Besides, I felt that since we had been preaching to the people that Christ could heal, if I could not show them that I trusted the Lord for myself, that part of our preaching would have been in vain.

The family with whom I was staying was in a dilemma. They knew little of divine healing, except what we had preached. All evidence seemed to show that I was rapidly getting worse, and that unless something was done, I would die in their home. In such an event they reasoned, perhaps correctly, that they would be in trouble with the health authorities. To them, there seemed to be no alternative: Either a physician must be called, or they dare not keep me in their home.

Fortunately, Dr. John G. Lake, who at that time was in San Diego, sent word for me to be brought to his home. I shall be forever grateful for his kindness and hospitality. The 16-mile ride to San Diego was agonizing, although the driver was as careful as possible. Dr. Lake, who had prayed for tens of thousands and had seen multitudes delivered, prayed for me each evening. Nevertheless, it seemed that nothing could stop the progress of the affliction, which had now reduced me to extreme helplessness. Though I hated to think of it, I had the recurring thought that death was approaching.

Gradually weakening in body and racked with constant pain, I resigned myself to death. Yet I pondered the reason for all that had happened to me. Why should I be cut off at the very beginning of my ministry? Why, in a few hours of time, must a telegram be sent to my mother with the words, "Your son passed away at such and such an hour"? I thought of the grief that would come to her. I had wanted to preach the Gospel more than anything else in the world. Now it appeared that my ministry would end abruptly. Was this the will of God?

But God was to show Himself — first, through His Word. Sister Lake had been kind enough to give me some typed sermons by her husband on the subject of healing. As I read those messages, my attention was taken off my suffering and placed on the power of the risen Christ. As I read, I began to feel the moving of faith in my soul. Certain Scriptures came to me with force and vividness. The words quoted by Peter in Acts 10:38 concerning Jesus, "who went about doing good and healing all who were oppressed by the devil," left a deep impression upon me. Again in Luke 13, when Jesus healed the woman bent over, He showed that the infirmity was caused directly by the binding power of Satan (vs. 16). It came to me that it was not the will of God that I die, but rather the will of the devil. It was Satan who would be pleased if he could end my ministry before its time.

Another Scripture came to my attention. It was Mark 11:22-24 — still my favorite passage today. The words, "whatever things you ask when you pray, believe that you receive *them*, and you will have *them*," (vs. 24) fascinated me. A light was dawning, and I began to understand the difference between passive and active faith. Here was a direct warrant for my immediate healing — if I would dare to accept it.

I could wait no longer. I rang an emergency bell beside my bed. A nurse in the household came and asked what I wanted. I replied rather unceremoniously that I wanted my clothes so that I could get up. I do not remember her answer, except that she hesitated, perhaps not knowing whether I was in my right mind. However, faith had fired my soul, and I was insistent. "Come," I said, "you have been praying for my healing. Believe your own prayers and bring my clothes."

Not knowing what further to answer, the lady decided to humor me and brought my clothes. How I got into them I do not know, for I was very weak, and though the cramps had lessened, they had not ceased. But my thoughts were no longer on my pains, but upon the living reality of the promise of God. I knew I was healed!

I had lost 25 pounds, and my clothes hung upon me grotesquely, but I gave this no consideration. As my feet touched the floor, I began to praise the Lord for healing. That very instant, my cramps vanished! And for the first time in many days, I felt the sensation of hunger. I sat down to a hearty meal — to the astonishment of everybody except the Lake family, who were used to seeing miracles take place!

I was healed indeed! But there was one thing that God showed me about my healing that I have never forgotten. If God could heal me after I had been so close to death, how much more could He deliver and *protect* me from sickness. It was plain to me that God desired to fulfill His promise by keeping me free from sickness. And so for many years, I and my family have proven that the Lord is not only the Healer of our disease, but that He can keep the plague from us. He has not failed us, and we can fully recommend Christ as the Healer for every family.

I learned two great lessons:

1. Faith is an act. After prayer is made for healing, there is a time to act upon the Word of God. Deliverance came to me at the moment that I acted upon the Word of God.

2. Though it is wonderful to be healed, it is better to be delivered from sickness before it overtakes us. The Word of

God clearly teaches that divine health rather than divine healing is God's plan for the believer (Ex. 15:26).

Mother Healed of Cancer

For about ten years after that first healing, I enjoyed the blessings of health, rarely experiencing anything more than the discomfort of a cold. Then one day, while I was some 3,000 miles from home, I received a letter from my father. Mother usually did the writing, so when I saw that the letter was written in Father's handwriting, I knew something was wrong. Mother was desperately ill. Examination proved that she had that most dreaded disease, cancer! What terror that word strikes in the heart of many people!

A physician recommended an immediate operation which would have been quite expensive, with no more promise than a brief postponement of the inevitable. But Mother, who had great faith in God, determined to trust Him for healing.

I was far from home. I wanted to go to mother's bedside, but it was during the depression, and I had no money. I drove to an old school house. Some of the windows were broken, and if my memory serves me correctly, the door hung on one hinge. Kneeling by a bench, I laid my Bible down and opened it to one of the great promises of God: "Whatever things you ask when you pray, believe that you receive *them*, and you will have *them*" (Mk. 11:24). I did not pray long. It seemed that God's power was all around me. I said, "O God, although mother is 3,000 miles away, You have all power. I have prayed for others and they have been healed; now mother's life is at stake. At this moment I believe that Your power is destroying that cancer and that she shall live." When I arose, an assurance came to me that deliverance had come!

Three or four days later, I went to the post office again and found that an air mail letter awaited me. It was in mother's handwriting this time. And standing in the post office lobby, I hastily tore open the letter. Down the page I could read the words, "Hallelujah! ... Praise the Lord! ... God has done a miracle. ... The cancer is gone!"

About the time that I had been praying in the school house, two ladies came to Mother's home. One was a woman of faith; the other's faith was not very strong. As they waited on the Lord in prayer, suddenly mother said, "Something is taking place; I believe I am healed." One of the ladies ran out into the kitchen crying and saying, "Poor Effie! Poor Effie! She's going! One of my relatives felt the same way, and he died the next day. They all think they are getting better just before they die!" But mother said, "No, this is the touch of God." Soon she got out of bed, went to the bathroom and threw up the cancer. She was indeed gloriously healed.

A few months later, she made a trip to California to testify to friends and relatives. I met her there. What a thrill it was to know that God had done the miraculous, and faithfully fulfilled His promise!

The lessons God taught me in this experience were:

1. When a deadly disease strikes, do not panic. You cannot have both faith and fear. Do not look at the symptoms and allow fear to strike your heart. Look at the Word of God, and let it inspire you to believe.

2. Faith operates instantly and at any distance. At the moment that I prayed and believed God for Mother, healing came to her, though she was 3,000 miles away. If there is not someone who has faith present to pray for you, do not despair. God has prepared resources for every situation.

3. After you are healed, stand on the promise, and believe that God will keep you healed. I have heard of cancer returning to some after they were delivered. This is as unnecessary as a person backsliding after God has saved his soul.

Marriage

The time came that I married Freda, a young lady who lived in Portland, Oregon. She was an excellent Christian and had great faith in God. However, she had not been taught strongly in the truths of divine healing. It was not long before she was tested in believing God for healing and health, even as I had been. But I will let her tell her own story.

Chapter Two

Our Family Doctor

Every family needs a good physician, for it is doubtful that anyone can go through this life without needing help at one time or another. Let me introduce you to our Family Physician — Jesus.

Shortly after Gordon and I were married, we went to Billings, Montana, to start a new church. With the work small, and having mostly untrained helpers, I found myself in the role of song leader, Sunday School superintendent, young people's president, janitor, etc. Besides this, Gordon and I were going from house to house daily, passing out flyers and inviting the townspeople to our services.

It was unseasonably rainy, with pools of standing water. After leading the singing each night, I would come from the platform, many times perspiring. I would sit on the crude benches, with my feet on the wet sawdust and the atmosphere dripping with humidity.

I developed a heavy chest cold with intermittent coughing. When my weight dropped to 94 pounds, Gordon decided I needed a rest, so he drove me back to my mother's in Portland, and he returned to Billings. Ten days passed, and one morning while attempting to pick up a light footstool, I fell on top of it. My sister put me back to bed and then weeping, told me that the whole family was certain that I had tuberculosis (TB), but they had not wanted to tell me.

The Dreaded Tuberculosis!

Tuberculosis — what a horrible word! I, too, was afraid that I had it, but I had not let myself think about it. But now my sister intimated that I was its victim. Could it be true?

At my family's insistence, my lungs were X-rayed. The best lung was entirely spotted with TB; the other was so full of liquid that it showed up only as a blur. The doctor's remedy was to spend one year in bed, either in a sanitarium or wherever I could get constant and good care. Perhaps I would recover. My youth was about the only thing in my favor. What a bleak future for a bride of a few months!

Gordon's parents lived in Zion City, Illinois, where they had seen many miracles under Dr. Dowie. They called Gordon with the news. Having received the message, he got into his car and drove the 1,000 miles back to Portland, stopping only along the side of the highway to get a few winks of sleep.

Standing by my bed with real faith and determination, he encouraged me in the Lord. He suggested I spend the remainder of the day preparing my heart, and then he would pray for my healing.

I wept and prayed before the Lord, confessing any unbelief and asking God to erase any sin of omission. I John 3:21 was quickened to my soul: "If our heart does not condemn us, we have confidence toward God."

I felt no sense of condemnation. I was now ready for prayer. Gordon prayed a few minutes with me, and then we began thanking God for answering us. No immediate change was apparent, but I stood on the healing promises. I got up, walked around for a little while, then lay down again. I repeated this several times during the day. By the third day, we were on our way back to Billings, Montana! Within a month I had regained most of my strength and was able to resume my duties at the church and in my home.

Through the years, by taking a short rest period each afternoon, I have been able to lead a more than active life with many demands upon my time and strength. How happy I am today that in Satan's first all-out attack to cut my life short, I turned my case over to our Family Doctor, Jesus, and I have never had a recurrence of TB.

"Christ has redeemed us from the curse of the law" (Gal. 3:13). And Deuteronomy 28:22 tells us that part of this curse is consumption or TB. Praise God!

In 1940, our first baby, Carole (Shira), was born. She was a chubby, nine-pound picture of health. How happy Gordon and I were. But on the second day, as I placed my hand under her head, I was startled to feel a knot as large as a fifty-cent piece protruding quite badly. I had a feeling that this could be something very serious. But doubt gave way to faith as we daily thanked the Lord for the answer. Then I forgot about it.

One day long afterward as I was washing her hair, imagine my joy when I checked her head and could find not even a trace of the growth. Again, our Family Physician won the case!

When Carole was two, I began to develop a slight itching and burning on my body. We were in evangelistic work and constantly on the go. Many times if our affliction is not grave enough to hinder our daily routine, we do not seriously take the matter to the Lord. But as the weeks passed, I was feeling real discomfort — so much so that my sleep was interrupted, and many times in my waking moments, I would have to grit my teeth from sheer distress. I told my husband that unless God intervened, I would have to stop ministering. A nurse friend of ours said it sounded like cancer to her, and suggested I have an examination immediately.

That night, Brother Lindsay announced that we would have a healing service later in the week and asked those who wished prayer to spend the next two days in fasting. So for two days I closed myself in with God. Then I went into the prayer line. No feeling, no change. Only God's promises. But that was enough! During that night, as each attack came upon me, I rebuked the devil in the Name of Jesus. As the morning rays burst through my window, sweet relief had come, and I had the assurance that the victory was won. The Great Physician was present, and I am still healed today!

Cross-Eyes

In 1943, Gilbert, our oldest son, was born. After a few weeks, when his beautiful, large, brown eyes should have normally begun to focus, we noticed that they did not. Day after day as we watched him, we realized that his eyes were hopelessly crossed. At the age of 2, the pupil of one eye would often slide behind the bridge of his nose so that only the white would show. Many advised treatments or an operation. It was a long battle. I am sure that several thousand times we thanked the Lord for the answer. Today, when we tell strangers about the great victory, it is hard for them to believe it, but we have photographs to prove it. We made contact with the Divine Optometrist! You shall "through faith and patience inherit the promises" (Heb. 6:12).

The Car Accident

One night as we were returning home from church, I heard the rear door of our car open. Just as I turned my head, I saw 5-year-old Carole lose her balance as she attempted to close it. Seated in the front and holding Gilbert, I was unable to grab her as she fell out of the open door with a shrill cry when our car turned a corner.

Slamming on the brakes, Gordon reached her first. There she lay, whimpering on the pavement. She had slid along the road on the side of her face, and it was a mass of blood. We picked her up and rushed her to our home. By now she was shaking as though she would go into convulsions. She was bleeding internally and passing blood through her mouth. Needless to say, we called mightily on our God. All night, her father kept a vigil over her. She never suffered any ill effects nor scars. By one week later, when we attended a fellowship meeting at the church of Gordon's sister and brother-in-law, Rev. and Mrs. L.D. Hall, her face was nearly entirely healed, with new baby skin covering the bruises. The Master Surgeon had done a beautiful piece of plastic surgery!

Angelic Protection

When Gilbert was four years old, we lived in the lovely mountain resort of Ashland, Oregon, in a parsonage next door to a large gas station and garage that serviced huge, cross-country vans. One day, Gilbert was kneeling on the sidewalk, tying a toy to the rear of his tricycle.

Suddenly, as the station attendant watched, a large truck began backing right in Gilbert's direction. The attendant shouted loudly, but due to the noise of the motor, the trucker failed to hear him and kept right on backing. The attendant threw his hands over his face, feeling certain that the child would be crushed to death. But in that split second, the driver, for some unknown reason, threw on the brakes.

The service employee ran to the side of Gilbert, who was complaining that "That old truck tore my stocking." The truck had torn the sock from his foot, but left him unharmed! A few more inches, and he could have met death. How happy we were that we had committed our child at the beginning of that day to Him Whose eye never slumbers nor sleeps.

A Deadly Carbuncle

Having resigned our church in Ashland to begin publication of *The Voice of Healing*, we found ourselves living in the deep South — lovely Shreveport, Louisiana.

Now that the children were in school, we felt it best for me to stay at home with them during the school year. Gordon often traveled out of town on speaking engagements. On one trip to Baltimore, he had to sit up most of the night in a drafty airport waiting room. The next night he was up until almost dawn helping a fellow minister. He noticed a soreness in his neck, which became steadily more painful in the next several days.

By the time Gordon was to return home, his neck was giving him serious trouble! At Memphis, Tennessee, he stopped by a doctor's office for an examination. The doctor diagnosed it as a carbuncle at the top of the spine, and urged him to go to the hospital at once for an operation. Gordon told him that it was necessary for him to complete his trip to Shreveport. Only with the promise that he would see a doctor immediately did the doctor reluctantly release him. My husband assured him that upon his arrival home, he would get in touch with his *Family Doctor* without delay.

When I arrived home from the office that day, I found him lying on the sofa, his face drawn in pain. I did not perceive the full impact of his condition at once. We prayed, but for several days, the back of his neck continued swelling and the carbuncle took on an ominous dark reddish hue. Friends who dropped in intimated that it had gone into blood poisoning. Another very dear friend called a wonderful Christian doctor, who advised an operation at once due to the danger of spinal meningitis setting in because of the location of the carbuncle.

The first few days at home, Gordon urging kept me to bring a medical book from the office so that he could read the information under the word *carbuncle*. I read it at the office: "A very painful and dangerous infection ... often in the nape of the neck ... causing great exhaustion from the poisoning ... death often follows." I decided right then and there that he did not need that kind of encouragement, so I neglected to bring it each night.

Gordon stopped talking, keeping his face to the wall most of the time. We wondered if he should go to the hospital. He chose to stay at home. The doctor suggested I put hot packs on his neck to give some relief. This I did, desperately clinging to God. Finally, after what seemed an eternity of blackness, the light began to shine through. The witness was born in our hearts, and we knew God had heard. Within a few hours, the carbuncle took on multiple heads, all of which seemed to break at once, releasing a tea-cup of infection. Four days later he was in the house of the Lord, magnifying the Great Deliverer!

"Your Boy's Right Eye Is Blind!"

In 1952, we moved *The Voice of Healing* offices to Dallas, which was the commercial center of the South — an ideal location for evangelists and the missionaries passing through. We settled into our house, put the children into school and became busily involved with our Lord's work.

Then after dinner one night, I received a telephone call from the school nurse concerning our youngest child, Dennis, now 8. She said that she had been observing Dennis' right eye for a period of six weeks, which on first examination appeared to be nearly blind. Since children that age sometimes feign blindness, especially if they see someone in the class with a new pair of glasses getting a lot of attention, she told me that she waited for several weeks and then checked him again.

Pretending to have forgotten which one was the bad eye, she said to him, "Now, let's check the good eye first," as she covered the left eye. Immediately he called her attention to the fact that the left eye was the good eye. She said she looked at his record with a pretended rebuke, "I have the card right before me. You are wrong." Again he remonstrated. So, convinced of his truthfulness, she once more made a thorough check.

The nurse said that beyond a shadow of a doubt, Dennis was nearly blind in the right eye. Had he been hit by a ball? Did he fall and hit it on something? We were at loss to know what might have caused it! She urged us to have his eyes X-rayed, for it could be something serious. Immediately I was reminded of a friend who shortly before had lost the sight of one eye because of tumors! They removed the one eye, and hoped the other would not be affected. Could this be the case with my child? Was total blindness awaiting him?

I tested the eye myself and found that it was blind, just as the nurse had said. I quickly ran to Gordon, who quietly said that we would trust God. He wanted to spend a few days waiting on God before praying for Dennis. One Sunday night the children and I attended a revival held by one of our deliverance evangelists at a Full Gospel church. When the prayer line was forming, I caught Dennis' attention as he sat on the front row. He appeared to be about half asleep as I nodded for him to get into the line. He shook his head "no" several times. As I prayed silently, I saw him get up slowly and make his way to the rear of the church, as by now the line had become very long. Only one tiny girl was behind him.

By the time the evangelist prayed for all those people, he was very weary. When he came to Dennis, he quickly said, "God, heal this little boy," and passed him on. Being quite human, I was disappointed. I thought, "The evangelist didn't even ask what was wrong with him, and what a short prayer!" However, as we drove home, I felt a rebuke from the Lord for having felt the way I did, so I determined not to make a negative statement.

As we stepped inside the house, I asked Dennis, "Did the Lord heal you?" As if surprised that I would ask such a superfluous question, he replied, "Yes." I took him away from the rest of the family, covered his good eye, and pointed to a large number on the calendar. Without any difficulty he read the figures. Next I picked up my Bible. He was able to read it perfectly. Then I tried him on a testament with very small print. He could read very little.

Then, in the presence of the family, we went through the same tests. We praised God for what He had done. Turning to Dennis I said, "Now tomorrow morning before you go to school, we'll let you read out of the small testament." His vision was some improved by the next morning. The second morning, he missed only a few words, and on the third, praise God, he could see every letter clearly!

By this time, Dennis had been transferred to a new school that had been built about four blocks from our home. Knowing that the new nurse would have all the old records, I made an appointment with her to have Dennis' eyes checked. This she did, saying he had 20-20 vision! But when she pulled out his card, she was not a little puzzled. "What's happened here?" she exclaimed. I then testified to his healing, but she flatly refused to believe, saying "Those things don't just happen. It must have been a temporary blindness that corrected itself." How sad that some will not give glory to God.

Next I called the first nurse. I told her that Dennis' test showed he now had 20-20 vision and how he was healed. With gratitude for my calling her, she said, "Isn't that wonderful! I believe every word of it!"

Our Family Optometrist had come to the rescue!

The Mumps

In 1954, we sold our home so that we would have funds to build The Christ For The Nations printing plant to economically print millions of deliverance books and magazines. We moved our family into a downstairs apartment at the office. Moving is always a big job, especially with three children. Wearily, I climbed into bed at the close of that Memorial Day and fell into a sound sleep. The next morning I awoke feeling quite rested and praising God for the sweet peace that came as a result of having done what we felt God wanted us to do.

I had been awake only a few minutes when Gilbert came into the room, his face badly swollen. When I asked him what the trouble was, he said, "It might be the mumps. I've been playing across the street with Butch, and you know, he's had them for two weeks."

No, I didn't know that Butch had the mumps! Here was the editor's family, living in the quarters of Christ For The Nations and down with the mumps! Satan just would not win with this sort of strategy. An indignation came over Gordon and I as we prayed. Within a few hours, the swelling had gone down, his fever left, he ate normally and played all day, while we sang the praises of God. Our Specialist in childhood diseases had brought the cure!

Several weeks passed, and Gordon was again out of the city. One day I noticed that my jaws were giving me trouble as I chewed. The discomfort increased as time passed. On Sunday night, I returned from church to find I had a bad headache. Thinking I could sleep it off, I went right to bed. After a few hours, I awoke with a raging fever. My neck was very sore and I knew that I had picked up Gilbert's mump germs.

All alone, I got on my knees in bed and served notice on the devil that he had lost the first battle, and that according to God's Word, he was about to lose the second. Again and again I quoted the promises of God out loud while the children slept soundly on in the next room. Finally I fell asleep, and when I awoke, I was wringing wet with perspiration. The fever had vanished and I was well! Our Family Physician, Who is never too tired, never too busy, nor out of His office, made a house call in the middle of the night, and I was healed.

"He Who Dwells in the Secret Place"

When Gilbert was 15 years old, he was returning home from high school one afternoon, with a group of boys. All of them began running for a bus, which had stopped for them on busy Jefferson Street. Gilbert was in the lead and failed to see a car that was coming very rapidly. All cars in the second lane of traffic had already stopped, but the man in the third lane did not see the boys.

At that moment when Gilbert saw that he was going to be hit, he gave a desperate leap. The car miraculously missed him, but caught the trumpet that he was carrying, hurling it clear across the wide intersection. Strangely enough when he picked up his horn, neither it nor the case were damaged in any way.

When he told us about it, we reminded him that he had been dedicated to the Lord as a child. We also recalled that the night when he received his trumpet: Our whole family knelt in prayer and dedicated it to the Lord. How wonderful and true are the words of the Psalmist: "For He shall give His angels charge over you, to keep you in all your ways. In *their* hands they shall bear you up" (Psa. 91:11,12).

How do others live without Him? I wonder. Many don't; they go to premature graves. Even some Christians' lives are cut short through lack of knowledge of God's healing power. I feel it would be criminal to know the message of divine healing and not share it with a dying world.

In the 20 years of our marriage, not including when our three children were born, we spent perhaps a total of $25 for doctor bills, such as shots when we were going into a foreign country, etc. But you can see that Satan did not leave us unchallenged. What a different story from the conversation I once heard in a crowded supermarket.

Said one man to another, "You know, most of my check for the past year has gone to the doctor." To which the other replied, "That's my complaint. My family has had nothing but doctor and hospital bills all year, until I feel like turning my whole check over to the doctor each week, no questions asked. He gets it anyway. You might say, I'm just working to support the doctor."

True, doctors perform many wonderful services, and with much of the world having little knowledge of God's promises of healing, they do a vital work. But how much better it has been for our family, to have been able to invest our resources in the spreading of the Gospel and the salvation of souls, laying up treasures in heaven. By having our personal Physician, many times we have been spared the pain of operations, long treatments, and the associated high costs. We can say from experience that God "forgives all your iniquities ... heals all your diseases!" (Psa. 103:3)!

Gordon

I do not think that I need to add to my wife's testimony, except to say that it is all true. Divine healing works! I will, however, summarize a few of the lessons that we have learned from these experiences. While it is true that we have had some severe tests, nevertheless, with few exceptions, we have enjoyed uninterrupted health. We can truthfully say that sickness has had a very minor role in our lives. When it has come, we have found that invariably Christ, the Great Physician was there to deliver us. Our chief interest in recording these things is to help others to likewise enjoy the great benefits of divine health. It is really much easier to receive and maintain the blessing of health than it is to be constantly seeking healing from this or that affliction after it has become entrenched. I will briefly note a few of the important lessons we learned from our experiences.

1. In the case of Freda being struck down with tuberculosis, it was apparent that she had been working beyond her strength. Many Christians do the same. Under the burden of the ministry, many pastors and pastors' wives overwork, failing to get proper rest. As a result, they have a breakdown. That was the case of Epaphroditus (Read Phil. 2:25-30).

   We rejoiced in Freda's great deliverance, which came with spectacular swiftness considering the seriousness of her condition. But we also realized that she must take proper care of her body. From then on, each afternoon she set aside a short period in which she completely relaxed. The result has been that she has been able to do much more, and do it well, than she would have been able to without the rest.

2. In the case of Freda's cancer symptoms, there was no apparent change immediately after she was prayed for. Had she not been instructed, she could have said, as do countless numbers, "Well I didn't get healed this time, but I'll try again." Had she confessed such unbelief, she would not have received deliverance. But by reckoning God's Word was true, that the work was done, and by confessing faith instead of unbelief, her healing came and the symptoms never reappeared.

3. In the case of Gilbert's crossed eyes, we had to stand on God's promise a long time, but finally the answer came.

Gilbert's eyes, while not as strong perhaps as the eyes of some people, have nevertheless experienced a most wonderful miracle.

4. In regard to the accidents, or near accidents, that happened to our children, we make this comment: Christian parents should not let a day pass without putting their family into the hands of the Lord. "The angel of the LORD encamps all around those who fear Him, and delivers them" (Psa. 34:7). We cannot be on the alert 24 hours a day, but we can put our family into the keeping of Him Who "neither slumbers nor sleeps" (Psa. 121:4).

5. In the healing of Dennis' blind eye, an important truth is brought out. Jesus said, "They will lay hands on the sick, and they will recover" (Mk 16:18). Yet the average person does not believe he can be healed, if only this simple command is carried out. He wants to relate in full detail all his symptoms, both real and imagined. After that, he wants a long prayer made. If the evangelist does not do it in just that way, he is disappointed and may make no effort to believe. Dennis, however, believed that when the evangelist touched him, he would be healed. And that is exactly what took place.

Now concerning my own healing from the deadly carbuncle which came when it seemed that I despaired of life. I shall give my testimony in the words I used when writing the story a few days after the miracle of healing took place.

What to Do When Death Strikes

In relating this experience, I do so, trusting that I will give help and encouragement to others who may have a desperate encounter with the enemy. For a quarter of a century, I have enjoyed almost uninterrupted health, and on several occasions when sickness has attempted to secure a foothold in our home, God miraculously intervened and delivered us from all the works of Satan. I say this not boastfully, but as one who is humbly grateful for God's grace and mercy which He has always seen fit to extend to us.

I was engaged in some important business in the East, which required my staying up very late. On some nights, I slept very little. This was nothing new to me, since 2 a.m. had ordinarily been the time I retired.

The Devil Strikes Unawares

A day or two after I began this business trip, I became aware that a boil of some kind was forming on the back of my neck. Boils are usually inconsequential incidents, and I hardly gave the matter a passing thought. The next day, however, I noticed that the swelling was not the same as that of an ordinary boil. Had I been home, I certainly would have followed my usual pattern of action when any kind of sickness seemed to threaten: To wait upon God until I feel that I have dominion over the portending trouble. But I was at the business part of my journey, and the matters I was dealing with were occupying all my time and attention. My mistake was a common one — people usually do not get serious when an affliction threatens until the thing becomes securely entrenched.

Concluding my business on Friday, I found myself at the airport in Washington, D.C., a little after midnight, standing by for possible space on an airline headed West. It was at this time that I realized something was seriously wrong. The boil now extended over a space of several inches in width and was quite painful.

I was fortunate to get a plane that took me as far as Memphis. But arriving at the city, I was too weak to proceed further, and so remained overnight in a hotel. By morning, I found that the infection had spread across my entire neck, and was extremely hard and painful when touched.

I Learned the Seriousness of My Condition

While waiting for a plane, I determined to find out just what the trouble was, making inquiry of a local physician. He took a brief glance and his face paled. Looking at me earnestly, he said, "Sir, I am sorry to tell you this, but this is a most serious infection — it is a carbuncle, and has developed to the point where it is going to give you great trouble; such things often result in ..." His voice trailed off, and then continued, "The infection is near your spinal cord, and can result in spinal meningitis." He spoke decisively. "You must have medical treatment at once."

I was weak and exhausted and in no condition to argue. So I said, "Doctor, I thank you for this information, but I will do nothing until I reach Shreveport. My plane leaves shortly." The physician was a kind man, and he was convinced I did not realize the gravity of the situation. He admonished, urged, cajoled, begged and almost threatened. But I was adamant. If this was a matter of life and death, then I must throw myself on the mercy of Jehovah Rapha, the Lord our Healer. Weak as I was, I did not feel that I could convince him.

He looked at me again and, almost with tears in his eyes, said, "If you do not have the money, don't worry over that. Your life is more important than money." Of course, the money was not the object, and I could not but appreciate the kind solicitude of the physician.

But when the doctor saw that I would not undergo medical treatment in Memphis, he turned to me and said, "I'll let you go on one condition — that you call your physician as soon as you reach Shreveport." I replied, "Doctor, I promise you that the moment I get to Shreveport, I'll call on my Physician." I kept that promise, even before I got to Shreveport. I most earnestly called on my Physician — the Great Physician, the Sympathizing Jesus.

The Battle Begins

In Shreveport, the battle began. I believe that an answer from heaven came the first day, but due to an organized attack of the powers of hell, the result was not manifest immediately. Because of the part our organization plays in salvation-healing revivals, the devil evidently believed he could effect a damaging blow if he could get me out of the way. No man is indispensable, yet each of us is given a task that is peculiarly our own.

Having great confidence in the prayers of others, I sent out telegrams to several of my brethren containing the following words: "The devil has struck me with a serious infection. I am convinced as with Daniel, the answer has already been sent. Undoubtedly, this attack is tied up with the devil's attempt to frustrate the rapidly-growing revival around the world. Please hold on to God with me for the manifestation of complete deliverance. Gordon Lindsay."

I deeply appreciate all those who held faith with me, and those who visited and prayed with me. We are members of one body, and the prayers and faith of others are of great significance and importance.

The Battle Rages

For three days the battle raged. I could feel the terrific impact of spiritual forces in action — the carbuncle being the nerve center of the battle arena. In the natural, the issue seemed in doubt. But in the spiritual realm, God gave me peace. I could feel that the Spirit of God was raising up a standard against this menacing evil that was fighting for my life. The struggle went on for hours — sometimes in the middle of the night. After I had prayed for healing, I ceased begging or crying. I have often seen this method of begging or crying after prayer for healing used and it is worse than useless. I just kept praising God for the victory that I knew was surely mine.

I did one other thing. I searched my life carefully and asked the Spirit of God to turn the searchlight on anything that was displeasing to Him. An attack by the enemy should always be a means of drawing us closer to God. A great mistake, and one made too often, is that when Satan strikes, people begin to whine and say, "I don't know why this had to come on me."

An attack by the enemy may not indicate sin, but it often indicates that we have let the devil break down the hedge of divine protection somewhere, if only in our failure to obey the laws of rest, diet, health, etc.

When one is in severe pain, the greatest battle is to reject the false sensory knowledge that denies the promise of God. If not properly taught, one is almost certain to accept the verdict of the pain rather than praising God for the sure promise of healing and deliverance.

A Premature Victory

On Tuesday afternoon, I felt that victory had come. Simultaneously, the great swelling opened and the poison began to drain out. Every hour or so, my wife would put a fresh hot pack on the place of infection, and the draining continued. The pain had ceased, and at last, I could fully relax. God had graciously prevented the affliction from passing to any other part of my body — a remarkable exception to the normal and usual course of a carbuncle.

A Trick of the Enemy

I will admit that I was not prepared for the next development. Apparently Satan thought there was much at stake in the outcome of the battle and had no intention of retiring from the field until he had played his last card. My father and mother were visiting us at the time. Father, who was 78 years of age, had never been really sick in his life. He had led a very temperate life, and hardly knew what sickness was.

At one o'clock on Wednesday morning, Freda was applying cloths, for the poison was flowing out rapidly. I was completely relaxed. At that moment, my father came into the room. I thought perhaps he had come to see how I was, but one look at him and I knew something definitely was wrong. His face grimaced with pain. He informed us that his kidneys had locked, and I could see that he was in great agony. I also perceived that he was suffering so much he would not be able to get victory himself. Satan, frustrated, had apparently lashed out against him.

I was distressed. There was my poor old father, whose hands had soothed my brow many a time when I was in need as a child. He had waited on me more times than I can remember. Now he was in pain and suffering, begging me to pray for him. It was almost more than I could bear. I arose from the bed and with all my strength began rebuking the enemy, but my strength did not last long. Five or six times I arose to rebuke the enemy, but at last I fell back utterly exhausted. Father recovered, for which we praise God!

Had I Lost My Healing?

As for me, I fell into a fitful sleep of exhaustion. I would see hallucinations, and time after time, I would wake with a sudden start. At length in the afternoon, Freda came and looked at the carbuncle. It was red and angry, had increased in size, and worse — it had completely closed up. She had little to say. Her face was solemn, and the thought came to me, "Had I, through this over-exertion, lost my healing?"

Temptations which are nothing in normal times loom large when one's strength is completely exhausted. Yet, in my extremity, God helped me. I grimly determined to refuse to accept anything but that God had healed me. That was my decision, live or die, sink or swim.

Having no strength to pray, I picked up the Bible and read the story of Hezekiah's sickness unto death. He too had been afflicted with a terrible boil or carbuncle, and when he had inquired of the Lord, the prophet had brought him word, "'Set your house in order, for you shall die and not live' " (Isa. 38:1). I read on. I saw how Hezekiah had turned his face to the wall and had pleaded with God to spare him and give him additional years of life. As a result of his prayers, God sent him a message that he would recover and live 15 additional years.

I read further. Though Hezekiah had been told he would be healed, apparently the symptoms were still there — the hideous, terrible, death-dealing carbuncle was still on his body. The pain was there, and seemingly nothing had changed. To stimulate his faith, he asked God for a sign. He was given his choice of whether the shadow would go forward or backward 10 degrees on the sundial of Ahaz.

Looking objectively at Hezekiah, we would probably think that the miracle of the shadow moving on the sundial would be far beyond the mere healing of a carbuncle. But as I lay there in bed, I could understand how that terrible, painful boil loomed larger to Hezekiah than anything else. He asked that the shadow go backward 10 degrees in order to give him faith for the healing of this affliction, of which as yet he saw no signs of abatement.

Not in a moment but gradually, as I lay there, I realized that God had given me a greater sign than He gave to Hezekiah — the sign of the Son of Man, "By His stripes we are healed" (Isa. 53:5). And "He Himself took our infirmities and bore our sicknesses" (Matt. 8:17). And when He did this on Calvary, the sun did not just retreat 10 degrees, but it withdrew its light altogether! When Jesus died, darkness came upon the face of the entire land! Calvary is a sign to every sick person that Jesus has borne his sickness.

As I lay in bed praising God for healing, it seemed that a new strength came to me, and a voice seemed to say, "Do not doubt your healing." I fell asleep, believing that victory had come, and Satan was defeated. When I awoke in the morning, I found that the swelling was going down rapidly, and the poison was again flowing from it. That was Thursday. By Monday I was back at the office working, and that evening I attended a church service. Hallelujah! Praise the Lord! Hezekiah went up to the house of the Lord on the third day. I believe that I could have gone on the third day also, but friends told me I had better wait another day.

My testimony is that of Hezekiah after he had been healed. "The LORD *was ready* to save me; therefore we will sing my songs with stringed instruments all the days of our life, in the house of the LORD" (Isa. 38:20).